Willi Sauer

HEIDELBERG

A Guide to Town and Castle

Heidelberg - Alte Brücke und Schloß   *nach Chapuy*

Text: W. Kootz

Edm. von König-Verlag, Heidelberg

Practical Information for Visitors

Information: Tourist information, D-6900 Heidelberg, at the Main Station, Postfach 1755, tel. (06221) 2 18 81, 2 13 41, open Mo.–Sat. 9 a.m. to 8 p.m., Sun. 2 p.m. to 8 p.m.

Tourist information, D-6900 Heidelberg, Mountain Railway Station Castle, tel. (06221) 2 96 41,

Tourist information at the bus-parking (Neckarmünzplatz), tel. (06221) 2 96 41

Mountain railway: Valley station at the "Kornmarkt"

Libraries: University library: Mo.–Sat. 11 a.m. to 12,

Municipal library (Stadtbücherei): 16, Kurfürstenanlage Mo.–Fr.

Federal Railway Inquiry-office: Tel. 2 32 46 11 a.m. to 5 p.m.

Camping: Heidelberg-Schlierbach, tel. 5 95 06, Ziegelhausen, tel. 5 08 42, Haide, tel. (06223) 21 11

Bicycles to hire: At the main station (summer months only)

Guided tours: Tourist information, tel. (06221) 2 96 41

Lost Property Office: 2, Vangerowstrasse, tel. 5 87 15

Change: On Sundays and Holidays in the main station 9 a.m.

Tourist information at the castle 9 a.m. to 6 p.m.   to 1 p.m.

Tourist information at the bus-parking (Neckarmünzplatz) 9 a.m. to 6 p.m.

Golf course: Golfclub Heidelberg, Lobenfeld, tel. (06226) 12 96

Indoor swimming-bath: 45, Bergheimer Strasse, 8 a.m. to

Post office: 6, Sophienstrasse, tel. 2 71 11   6 p.m.

Youth Hostel: Tiergartenstrasse, tel. 4 20 66

Police: 11, Rohrbacher Strasse, tel. 2 72 51

Sauna: Indoor swimming-bath, tel. 51 31, and: Am Czernyring, tel. 2 50 55

Service of motor-boats along the Neckar valley: At the Stadthalle, summer months: 9.30 a.m., 11 a.m., 2 p.m., 2.30 p.m.

Castle illumination: 3 to 5 times a year, inquire at Tourist inform.

Swimming-pools: Städt. Schwimmbad at the Zoo, and: Thermalbad, Vangerowstrasse

Coach sightseeing tours: At the Bismarck Square and the main station, 10 a.m. and 2 p.m.

Coach sightseeing tours round the town: At the Bismarck Square and the main station, 10 a.m. and 2 p.m.

Taxi: Tel. 3 76 76

Telephone-inquiry: 01 18 (West Germany), 0 01 18 (other

Tennis: Kirchheimer Weg, tel. 47 10 06   countries)

Theatre: Städtische Bühne, 4 Theaterstrasse, tel. 2 05 19, and: Zimmertheater, 112, Hauptstrasse, tel. 2 10 69

Tourist ticket: Travel agency and hotels

Tourist Information: At the main station

Rooms to let: Tourist information

Zoo: Tiergartenstrasse, 9 a.m. to 7 p.m., winter months: 9 a.m. to

Emergency Services   5 p.m., tel. 4 00 41

Police emergency call: Tel. 110 .

Fire brigade: Tel. 112

First aid, ambulance service: Tel. 2 14 54

View from the Philosophen Lane: Heidelberg Castle and Town with the Old Bridge, in background the Königstuhl (568 metres above sea-level).

"Old Heidelberg, thou fair one, thou town in honours rich..."

(Victor von Scheffel)

Heidelberg, Germany's oldest University Town is situated in a delightful setting on the banks of the river Neckar, where it spreads out into the broad plain of the Rhine. Innumerable poets of the Romantic age have praised Heidelberg's unique site with its fascinating maze of roofs between the "Old Bridge" and the famous Castle. Thus Heidelberg became the wellknown romantic town, "where you lose your heart". From the "Philosophen Lane" (Philosophen-Weg) you can enjoy the magnificent views over the whole town. Not being damaged during World War II Heidelberg has remained an attractive place for tourists from all over the world. Many traditional restaurants and inns are providing a solid hospitality. Due to its modern facilities for free time amusement and its convenient traffic conditions Heidelberg is an inviting place of interest.

Heidelberg's main objects of interest

Heidelberg Castle: Started in the 14th century, conquered and damaged in the 16th and 17th century. Romantic ruins with fascinating Renaissance façades (Ottheinrich Building, Friedrich Building) and gardens.

Great Vat: Biggest wine-vat of the world (55,345 gallons) built in 1751 for Karl-Theodor.

Old Bridge: Romantic stone-bridge dating from the 18th century with gate and towers built in the 13th century.

Church of the Holy Ghost: Church in the Gothic style, begun in the 13th century. Tomb of King Ruprecht I and his wife.

Ritter-inn: Patrician House with beautiful Renaissance façade.

Kurpfälzisches Museum: The Windsheim Altar of the Twelve Apostles by Tilman Riemenschneider.

Plaster-cast of the lower jaw of the "homo heidelbergensis" (about 550,000 years old), pre-historic finds. Palatine Collection.

University Library: Collection of valuable manuscripts, collection of Old German troubadour songs (Manesse Codex, 14th century).

Studentenkarzer (Student's prison): 1712–1914 with drawings and inscriptions left by its former inhabitants.

Philosophen Lane: Promenade half way up the Heiligenberg with a beautiful view over castle, town and Old Bridge.

Castle illumination: With fire-works held 3 to 5 times a year. Dates at the Tourist Information.

Sightseeing tours and showing rounds

Guided tour of the town: Tourist Information at the main station.

Coach tours round the town: Starting at Bismarck Square and main station at 10 a.m. and 2 p.m., taking about 2 hours.

Castle showing rounds: Daily 9 a.m. to 6 p.m. taking about 1 hour, including visit of the Great Vat. Starting-point at the Castle ticket-office.

Pharmaceutical Museum: Entrance at the ground-floor of the Ottheinrich Building. April to November 10 a.m. to 5 p.m., December to March Sat. and Sun. 11 a.m. to 5 p.m.

Kurpfälzisches Museum: 97, Hauptstrasse, daily (except Monday) 10 a.m. to 1 p.m. and 2 p.m. to 5 p.m.

Students' prison: 2, Augustinergasse (behind the Old University) 9 a.m. to 5 p.m.

University Library: At the corner of Grabengasse and Plöck, daily (except Sunday), 11 a.m. to 12 a.m., admission free.

Church of the Holy Ghost: Showing rounds daily.

Friedrich Ebert memorial: Pfaffengasse, daily (except Sunday) 10 a.m. to 1 p.m. and 2 p.m. to 5 p.m., Sundays 10 a.m. to 1 p.m., admission free.

Tiefburg: Handschuhsheim, Sundays 10.30 a.m. to 12.30.

Observatory: Königstuhl, by appointment only, tel. 4 14 52.

From the History of Heidelberg Town and Castle

About 550 000 a. Chr. n.	"homo heidelbergensis"—lower jaw bone, oldest human find in Europe, found near Heidelberg.
400 a. Chr. n.	Celtic ring walls on the Holy Mountain.
100 p. Chr. n.	Roman bridge and Roman citadel in Heidelberg-Neuenheim. Roman signal tower on the Holy Mountain.
769	The village of Bergheim was documented.
1155	Emperor Friedrich I Barbarossa bestowed the title of an Earl Palatine on his half-brother Konrad of Hohenstaufen.
1196	*"Heidelberch"* was documented for the first time.
1214	Heidelberg Castle was documented: Bishop Heinrich v. Worms gave Heidelberg village and Castle to Ludwig I of Wittelsbach.
1303	Two castles above the town were documented, one of them being situated on the Gaisberg (the present "Molkenkur") the other on the "Jettenbühl".

Lieselotte Palatine, a contemporary painting.

1329	Emperor Ludwig the Bavarian and his nephew Ruprecht I separated the Palatinate from Bavaria by the "Contract of Pavia".
1359	The Emperor bestowed the title of an Elector on the heirs of Ruprecht for all times.
1386	Heidelberg University was founded.
1400	Elector Ruprecht III was made German King (Ruprecht I Palatine). The Ruprecht Building and the Holy Ghost Church were begun.
1462	Elector Friedrich the Victorious won the battle near Seckenheim.
1534	The upper castle was destroyed by lightning.
1556—59	Otto Heinrich reformed Church and University. He set up the Ottheinrich Building (finest Renaissance façade north of the Alps).
1610—32	Friedrich V married the English Princess Elizabeth Stuart. He set up the English Building and laid out the famous "Palatine Gardens". In 1619 he was made King of

Bohemia (the "Winter King"). In 1620 he lost the "Battle at the White Mountain" at the beginning of the Thirty Years' War.

1618—48	During the Thirty Years' War three quarters of the Palatine population were killed.
1622	General Tilly besieged and conquered Heidelberg Town and Castle.
1623	The "Palatine Library" was displaced to Rome.
1633	Heidelberg was conquered by Swedish troups.
1634—35	Town and Castle were occupied by the Emperor's troups.
1648—80	Karl-Ludwig rebuilt the Castle and re-established the University.
1653	In the Palatinate people from Belgium, Switzerland, etc., built their new homes.
1671	Liselotte Palatine, daughter of Karl-Ludwig was married to the brother of Louis XIV, the French King.
1685	The Roman Catholic family of Pfalz-Neuburg gained the succession by inheritance.
1688	The Imperial Council turned down Louis XIV's claim, the French King's answer was a declaration of war. Heidelberg had to surrender.
1689	French troups under the leadership of General Melac destroyed the Castle completely, the town only in part. They also destroyed all the towns and villages in the Rhine valley.
1693	There was another French conquest. The town and castle fortifications were blown up, the town was burnt down completely. Soldiers plundered and destroyed the tombs of the Electors in the Church of the Holy Ghost.
1720	Because of religious quarrels about the Church of the Holy Ghost, Karl-Philipp transferred his Electoral residence to Mannheim.
1742—99	Karl-Theodor built the Old Bridge, the Karl's Gate and Schwetzingen Castle. He started the renovation of the Castle.
1764	During the reconstruction a lightning-stroke destroyed some buildings so that the reconstruction was given up. The ruins fell into disrepair and were abused as a "quarry".
1803	The Duke of Baden re-established the University. It was called "Ruperto Carola".
About 1800	Karl Graf von Graimberg, a French emigrant, began the reconstruction of the Castle ruins and the establishment of a Palatine collection.

Heidelberg Castle

Motor tourists are advised to get to the Castle via the "New Castle Street" (Neue Schlossstrasse) starting from the "Corn Market" (Kornmarkt) or the "Castle Hill" (Schlossberg). There is a car park just in front of the Castle ruins. You may also park your car in the "Parkhaus Kornmarkt" and take the Funicular or even walk up the "Short Hill" (Kurzer Buckel) or the "Castle Lane" (Burgweg) which leads you through gloomy vaultings and past grey walls straight into the Castle yard. Near the "Charles Gate" (Karlstor) starts the "Friesenberg Lane" (Friesenbergweg), a pleasant foot-path to the Castle gardens. The nearer we get to the Castle the more our eyes are caught by the imposing red sandstone building. The construction was begun about 1300 and lasted 400 years as a whole. Later on ramparts, outbuildings and palaces in all styles from Gothic to High Renaissance were added to it. They give evidence of the power and love for the fine arts of Heidelberg's noble families. The visitor is given an interesting lesson about how the Electors lived in times that are long gone by.

Castle courtyard beginning on the left, the Friedrich Building, the Hall of Mirrors Building, the Bell Tower, the Ottheinrich Building, the Well House (on the right).

7

The Ruprecht Building

After reaching the Castle yard you should linger for a moment and enjoy the whole picture of the famous ruins. On the right you find the oldest part of the Castle, the Ruprecht Building, built by Elector Ruprecht III in the Gothic style. He also laid the foundation-stone of the Church of the Holy Ghost. The imperial eagle on the left hand side of the arms tablet symbolizes the royal dignity of Ruprecht who was also a German King from 1400 to 1470. In its claws the eagle holds the arms of the Palatine Lion and the Bavarian Rues. We also find these arms in a second tablet of arms,

The angel relief at the portal of the Ruprecht Building (15th century).

the Palatine Lion wearing a crown on its head. The inscription says that Count Palatine Ludwig V renewed the building. This coat of arms was added to the tablet by Friedrich II in 1545 a year after Ludwig's death. At the entrance-gate can be found the famous Gothic relief with two angels holding a wreath of five roses which encloses a pair of compasses. The story goes that the beloved twin kids of the masterbuilder fell from the scaffolding. One night the dead children appeared as two angels in the unhappy father's dream. In the morning he found the wreath of roses from their grave at his bedside. According to another interpretation the wreath of roses symbolizes the many prayers of the religious Elector.

The Library Building

At the end of the west front of the Castle the Ruprecht's Building and the "Women's Building" (Frauenzimmerbau) form one line with the façade of the Library Building behind them. It used to be four storeys high and presents a beautiful Gothic bay window behind which in former times was a banqueting-hall.

The Women's Building and the Royal Hall

Before the deconstruction the two upper storeys held rooms of the ladies of the Court and the servants. In its long history the ground-floor was used as a banqueting-hall, a sculptor's workshop and a cellarman's workshop in which the Great Vat was constructed.

Being gravely damaged in the Thirty Years' War it was reconstructed, destroyed again and at last the ground-floor was roofed over by Karl-Theodor in 1767.

Today the "Königsaal" is a festival hall with about 700 seats.

The former Women's Building was pulled down to the ground-floor, the King's Hall was renovated. On the left of it is the Library Building with its Gothic bay-window.

The Friedrich Building

By the huge knight's statues at the façade, framed by columns and human and lion's heads, our attention is drawn to a high Renaissance building at the north side of the courtyard.

They are only copies of the statues by Sebastian Goetz from Chur in Switzerland. To shelter them from weather-beating the originals are shown in the interior of the Castle. The upper line is a gallery of the ancestors of the Wittelsbach family: Charlemagne, Otto of Wittelsbach, Ludwig II and Rudolf I. In the second horizontal line are engraved emperors and kings of the Wittelsbach House:

Ludwig the Bavarian, Ruprecht Palatine, Otto of Hungary and Christoph of Denmark. The most famous Counts Palatine are to be found in the window niches of the first upper floor: Ruprecht I, founder of the University, Friedrich the Victorious, Friedrich II, and Otto Heinrich, the builder of the "Mirror Hall" (Gläserner Saalbau) and the Ottheinrich Building. In the lower line, at last, between the windows of the Castle chapel, come the princes of the Palatine-Simmern-family: Friedrich III and Ludwig VI, Johann Kasimir, builder of the Vat Building and of the first Great Vat, and the builder of the Friedrich Building himself. The latin inscription says that in 1607 Friedrich, Count Palatine built this palace to the worship of God and as a comfort dwelling, decorated with many statues of his ancestors. Among Friedrich IV's assets was a diary in which he entered all his drunkennesses, e.g. on 9th June 1598: "Gestern wieder voll gewest" (I was drunk yesterday). To this refers an old drinking-song which is very popular among Heidelberg's students. The translation would be as follows:
"Count Palatine Friedrich furiously wallowed in his pillows, against all etiquette he shouted as loud as he could:
How did I get to bed last night?
May be I was drunk again."
No wonder he needed a crutched stick at the age of thirty and died only six years later.

The Hall of Mirrors Building

Finished in 1546, this early Renaissance building connects harmoniously the two richly decorated façades of the Friedrich and Ottheinrich Building. With its loggias, its staircase tower on the right and its projecting gabled house (with sun-dial) it is an excellent combination of the Gothic and Renaissance style. A festival hall in the first upper floor, which was fitted out with Venetian mirrors gave its name to the whole building. In 1764 this part of the Castle was destroyed by a fire, which raged three days and four nights. This fire also destroyed the neighbouring buildings except for the Castle chapel.

Between the arcades in the centre we find the arms of the builder, Friedrich II: the Palatine Lion, once golden with a red crown on black background, the Bavarian Rues, once silver and blue and the orb, golden on red background—which was granted to Friedrich II as a sign of dignity by Emperor Karl V in 1544, when Friedrich II was the highest official at his court. On the right and left hand are the arms of Friedrich's wife, Dorothea of Denmark.

The gorgeous courtyard façade of the Friedrich Building with its more than life-size statues of the builder Friedrich IV and his most famous ancestors of the House of Wittelsbach.

A memorial tablet reminds us of the French Count of Graimberg and his great efforts at the preservation of the Castle ruins. About 1800 he lived in the undestroyed part of this building.

The Ottheinrich Building

The most imposing building of Heidelberg Castle is the Ottheinrich Building. Its world-famed courtyard façade is a fine example of German Renaissance architecture. Innumerable elements of many countries in Europe were united by the masterbuilder so excellently

11

that they produced a full harmony of the various parts of the building with the ornaments and statues. Broad mouldings put a stress on the horizontal lines. The half columns, on the ground-floor Dorian, then Ionian and Corinthian devide each floor into five parts with two windows and one niche in each of them. The magnificent portal, in the form of a triumphal arch, is certainly unique in the world. The medallion with Ottheinrich's picture above the entrance, the arms and especially the inscription in Old German refer to the builder who was also a lover of the fine arts:

"Ott Hainrich von Gottes gnaden Pfalntzgraf bei Rhein.
Des heyligen Römischen Reiches Ertzdruchses und Churfürst,
Herzog in Nider und Obern Bayern."

The windows on the ground-floor are devided in the form of a cross with triangular gables on top. Copies from the Roman coins in Ottheinrich's collection are framed by cherubs playing on musical instruments. The tall statues in the lowest storey are Josuah, Hercules and David — heroes of the Old Testament. The meaning of the statues is explained to us in simple verses. In the niches of the first floor we find the five virtues: Strength (with a broken column), Faith (with the Bible in her hand), Charity (with children), Hope (with an anchor) and Justice (with scales and sword). The seven figures in the upper part of the façade are gods of antiquity: Saturn, Mars, Venus, Mercury, Diana and, at the top, sun and moon. The original statues by the Dutch sculptor Alexander Colin from Mecheln have been replaced by copies, like those of the Friedrich Building to save them from damage. In 1556, when Ottheinrich was made Elector for only three years there was only a small gap between the Ludwig Building and the Hall of Mirrors Building. So he pulled down the neighbouring Ludwig Building to the middle. At the base of the Ottheinrich Building we see that the foundations of the Ludwig Building remained unchanged and that its simple masonry reaches up to the outside staircase of the newer building. Thus the art-loving Elector gained a place for his palace. In the ground-floor on the right besides smaller rooms were the audience hall and the drawing-room of the heavy prince, on the left the "Emperor's Hall". The staircase towers of the other buildings were used to reach the upper floors.

The richly decorated Renaissance façade of the Ottheinrich Building with the mighty portal in the form of a triumphal arch.

The Buildings of Ludwig V

The arms at the staircase tower with the date of the year 1524 refers to Ludwig V, the great builder of the Castle. The southern wing of the Ludwig Building together with the neighbouring building completes the ring of buildings by the same builder around the Castle courtyard. Ludwig preferred unadorned simplicity, examples for which are the Library Building and the Women's Building. The only part of the court kitchen which still remains is the fireplace. The knights kitchen was at the south-east corner, the butchery and bakery were nearby. There is now an inn, the "Schloss Weinstube" in the first upper floor.

The columns of the "Well-House" (Brunnenhalle) are monoliths of granite. They were brought to Heidelberg from Charlemagne's palace in Ingelheim (near Mainz) and are most likely of Roman origin. The draw-well is over 20 metres deep (50 ft.) and was to provide the Castle with water in case of siege. In the Soldiers' Building—today the ticket office—the garrison had its guard-house.

The Castle courtyard in the 17th century, on the left the Women's Building, the Friedrich Building, the Hall of Mirrors Building, on the right of the staircase are the Ludwig Building and the domestic buildings (engraving by U. Krauss).

The Great Terrace (The "altan")

Walking through the arched passage of the Friedrich Building we find ourselves on the terrace with its bay-windows at the front corners. The foot-print in one of the flags is said to be left

Town side of the Castle before its destruction. On the right is the Thick Tower with the Theatre, next to it the English Building, on the left of the altan is the mighty arsenal, in front of it the Great Battery.

behind by a scorned lover who jumped out of the window in full armour. The Friedrich Building is the only one which has two decorated façades. The rear façade shows its magnificent beauty especially in the great Castle fireworks several times a year. Further to the right, the Wine Vat Building completes the façade behind the terrace. It contains the mighty oak vat with its capacity of 55,345 gallons, the biggest vat ever filled with wine.

On the other side we find the arched windows of the Hall of Mirrors Building and the octagonal Bell Tower which had been erected in four periods. First it had only one floor then it was no longer needed as a part of the fortification, so Ludwig V added to it another storey. Then followed two octagonal floors with a bell and at last another storey with a smaller diameter. In the arsenal—in front of the Bell Tower—the provision of war material was kept. After the Thirty Years' War another bastion was built in front of the arsenal: "The Charles' rampart" (Karlsschanze) and the "Charles' Tower" (Karlsturm) with its five floors. Together with the ramparts below the terrace and the roofed ramparts below the Thick Tower the Castle became unbesiegable from the town side.

Let us now enjoy the marvellous view over the town. There we find the mighty building of the "Church of the Holy Ghost" (Heiliggeist-kirche) (begun in the 15th century) with its Baroque tower and delicate turret and the Old Bridge (Karl-Theodor-Brücke) with its picturesque gate towers. The opposite banks of the Neckar are narrow and rise up to the wooded heights of the "Holy Mountain" (Heiligenberg). Before it spreads down into the Rhine Valley there is the "Bismarck Tower" (Bismarckturm) whereas the look-out tower is almost completely hidden behind trees. The Neckar leaves its narrow bed and spreads out in broad windings to the Rhine Valley.

The Castle seen from the look-out tower on the Holy Mountain. Below the high façade of the Friedrich Building is the look-out platform, the altan.

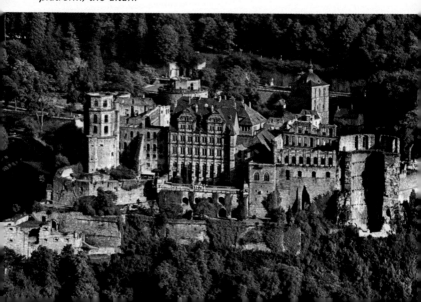

The Castle Interior

The interior of the Castle can only be visited by a guided tour. You get the tickets also including a visit to the Great Vat at the ticket-office near the Well House. The round takes about an hour, and if your time is very limited you should at least obtain a ticket to the world-famed cellar of the Great Vat.

The famous dwarf Perkeo, court fool and wine-loving guard of the Great Vat (by A. v. d. Werff).

The Great Vat

Its two predecessors, the 16th century "Kasimirtonne" and the richly decorated Karl-Ludwig-Vat built in the 17th century with their capacity of 125,000 litres and 195,000 litres were also imposing wine vat giants. They were surpassed, however, by the present building which was finished in 1751 by Karl-Theodor. Some 130 oak trunks were needed for a container 8.50 metres long and with a diameter of 7 metres. The platform can be reached by 42 steps. On the arms on the façade of the vat we find the letters C and T, the initials of the builder. On the wall stands the figure of the dwarf Perkeo. He was the Court Fool at the court of Karl-Philipp and Karl-Theodor and came from South Tyrolia.
Tradition says that Perkeo died after drinking a glass of water instead of the wine he was used to. Even today, the red-haired joker is the patron of Heidelberg's carnival and a symbol of the joyousness of live in the Palatinate. The clock beside the statue is one of Perkeo's jokes. If you pull the ring you can hear a wonderful "music". Try and find out yourselves what kind of clockwork it is. Left of the compasses and plane is a part of the wine-pipes by which the vat was connected with the festival hall, the King's Hall, where the average wine consumption was 2,000 litres a day! All Castle cellars together had a capacity of over 700,000 litres of wine.

The Great Vat (221,726 litres) with the initials of Karl-Theodor. Above the statue of Perkeo are the compasses and plane, on the left are the wine-pipes leading to the King's Hall.

How wine-loving the Castle's inhabitants must have been tells us a legend which says that Perkeo, the court-fool and guardian of the Great Vat consumed 18 bottles a day. All Castle cellars together had a capacity of over 700 000 litres of wine. The Great Vat was filled twice in its history and is said to be the World's biggest wine container.

Ruprecht Building–
Library Building–
King's Hall

Opposite the Castle ticket-office the round starts inside the oldest building. Besides a model which shows the Castle before its destruction we find a genealogical tablet of the Electors of the Wittelsbach family. Walking through the vaulted corridors we reach the King's Hall in the ground-floor of the Women's Building. It has been restored so perfectly that it can be used as a place for parties and theatre performances. Portraits of Electors and the wine-pump in the room on the left of the stage remind us of glorious times.

Magnificent fireplace inside the Ruprecht Building with inscriptions, medallions and arms of Friedrich II (1544–1556).

The renovated King's Hall inside the Women's Building is often used for concerts and theatre performances.

Ottheinrich, Heidelberg's reformer of Church and University.

The Domestic Building and the Ludwig Building

Partly unroofed there are only few remains of these buildings. At the fireplace below the high chimney of the kitchen oxen used to be roasted whole on a spit, water-pipes of stone supplied the Castle with water.

The Ottheinrich Building and the Hall of Mirrors Building

These two palaces were almost entirely destroyed by lightning-stroke in 1764. Only the façade of the Ottheinrich Building remains to the present day, the ground-floor has been secured by a temporary roof. In these rooms many art exhibitions take place throughout the year. Some of the original statues of the courtyard façade are protected against weather in the former dining-hall of the Ottheinrich

Hunting-carriage of Karl-Theodor (1742–1799)

Building and in the spacious "Königssaal". Here we also find Karl-Theodor's hunting-carriage and his gorgeous sledge with the initials of their owner which are also to be found on the façade of the Great Vat. The magnificent cross vaults of the King's Hall have been destroyed almost completely, only two Corinthian columns remain to the present day. The richly decorated portals give evidence of the art-loving builder. In the ground-floor of Ottheinrich Building the "German Pharmaceutical Museum" (Deutsches Apothekermuseum) was set up about 20 years ago. In the 19th century the French Count of Graimberg lived in the Hall of Mirrors Building. His great efforts at the preservation of the ruins all through his life are unforgettable.

The Friedrich Building

Since its completion in 1607 this palace has been lived in by the Electoral family. The first floor was restored in 1900 by Professor Karl Schäfer and is a perfect copy of the dwellings of Renaissance princes. Here we also find the original statues of the façade from the masterhand of Sebastian Goetz. The wooden door-frames and the ceilings are richly decorated. The precious gobelins (17th century) are from Aubusson (France). The larger one was manu-

factured after a painting by the French artist Charles de Brun, a court-painter of Louis XIV: the family of the Persian King Darius begging for mercy the victorious Alexander the Great.

Let us now enter the Elector's rooms. The iron plates of the fireplaces are richly decorated. On the green Nuremberg tiled stoves are scenes from the Bible. The most out-

Renaissance winding stairs in the Friedrich Building.

Corridor in the 2nd upper storey of the Friedrich Building with richly decorated stucco ceilings. Opposite the rooms are the original statues from the façade of the building.

Corridor at the courtyard side of the first floor the Friedrich Building with precious wooden ceiling and doors, on the right is a 17th century tapestry.

Electoral drawing—room in the Friedrich Building with Nuremberg tiled stove, precious door-frames and stucco ceilings.

standing object is a stove in light colours with golden lions in the socle. It was manufactured in the 17th century in Winterthur (Switzerland), besides Delft and Nuremberg a famous place for the fabrication of tiled stoves. On the plates are scenes and verses from the Old Testament. On the lisene tiles Man's life from childhood to death is described in pictures and verses. The stone winding stairs is decorated with ornaments which chiefly are to be found in wrought iron objects. Even the screws are a true

Beautiful tiled stove in a drawing-room.

Castle chapel in the Friedrich Building with Baroque altar.

imitation of iron material.

The Castle chapel in the ground-floor was originally a very simple place for the worship of God—according to the Calvinistic rules. The Roman Catholic Pfalz-Neuburg family however renewed the chapel in the 18th century. The Baroque altar dates from this time, the rest of the outfit and the paintings are by Professor Schäfer. Today the Chapel is often used for weddings. Lovers of heraldry are advised to pay attention to the numerous arms in the Chapel.

Below the statue of Christian of Denmark there is a coat of arms which consists of the arms of the Scandinavian countries. On the right of the altar we find the coloured arms of the Elector Jan Wilhelm and his wife from the noble family of Medici, who restored the Chapel in 1716. In the opposite corner of the Chapel is the remarkable statue of Johann Casimir. Apart from the "Winter King" he was the only Palatine Elector who also was a Knight of the Garter, a member of the famous English order with its well-known motto: "Honni soit qui mal y pense."

The Pharmaceutical Museum

In the ground-floor of the Ottheinrich Building the German Pharmaceutical Museum is located. Here are shown chemist's utensils, vessels, a significant collection of receptacles and medicaments. Most of them date from former centuries. There are even documents of medieval medical science with medicines of animal and human origin. This famous Museum is probably unique in the world. Tickets can be obtained in the Ottheinrich Building.

View into the lower storey of the Chemist's Tower: Laboratory in the German Pharmaceutical Museum with chemist's utensils and furnaces (16th century and 17th to 19th century).

View from the Gun Park at the mighty Gate Tower with the Gate Giants. In front, in the moat, the partly destroyed prison "Seldom Empty", above it the ruins of the Ruprecht's and Library Building.

The Gate Tower

Let us now turn to the entrance tower in the south of the picturesque Castle courtyard. This mighty gate fortress is the only tower of the Castle which has sustained all sieges almost undamaged. It is 52 metres high with the former Castle dungeon in the lower storeys. The entrance to the Castle was protected by four gates, a huge wooden lattice and a drawbridge. There is a hole in the vaulting above, through which the defenders could be drawn up into safety at the very last moment. Of the heavy iron ring in the gate tradition says that the Castle belongs to the person who can bite through it. After many people had tried in vain, a witch bit a little cleft into it.

In the stone bridge over the moat was a drawbridge the holes of which are still to be seen at the Gate Tower. The two storeys above the entrance were for the defenders and at the top were the rooms for the Tower guard. The formerly octagonal pointed roof was replaced by the present roof in the 18th century. The Gate Giants are the only decoration of the Gate Tower. The lions between them held the precious electoral coat of arms said to be of solid silver.

The Moat and the Guard House

The deep moat which was used for hunting in peace times was filled up with water in war times. Together with the walls which were seven metres thick it provided a good protection against military attacks from the mountain side. A smaller moat in front of the Guard House was protected by another two draw-bridges the footbridge of which is still to be seen.

The Gun Park and the Neighbouring Buildings

Behind the Bridge House we turn to the right and follow the path along the moat. At the corner is the smallest of the round towers with no more than loop-holes for rifles. It used to be a prison with the popular name "Seltenleer" which means "Seldom Empty". The "Elizabeth's Gate", a garden gate in the form of a triumphal arch was erected by Elector Friedrich V, the "Winter King" in 1615 as a birthday present for his 19 years old wife Elizabeth Stuart.

The "Elizabeth Gate", built in one night, was the entrance portal of the Gun Park on the western fortification.

The Gun Park with its beautiful flower-beds. In the background is the Thick Tower with the Electors' statues and the ruins of the Theatre, on the right is the English Building.

The "Gun Park" (Stückgarten) was built by Ludwig V. In war times it used to be a mighty fortification for the protection of the Castle. It was strengthened by the Thick Tower wich connected it with the northern fortification. The tower-shaped bastion in the middle of the western walls was five storeys high with a flight of winding stairs between them. In former times there even was a tunnel through which the defenders could get to the Thick Tower and the Castle interior. The walls of the Thick Tower are seven metres thick. With its diameter of 30 metres it seemed to be undestructible by attacks from the North and West. Nevertheless the French blew it up from the centre in 1689 like all the other round towers of the Castle. A few years before the Thirty Years' War the young Elector Friedrich V had diminished the efficiency of this fortress. He filled up the rondell partly and turned the Gun Park into a pleasure-garden for his English wife.

Between the Thick Tower and the Wine Vat Building the unadorned "English Building" (Englischer Bau) was erected. The upper part of the Thick Tower was pulled down and replaced by a sixteen-cornered storey with high windows. It was used as a theatre with about 500 seats. The view round from above must have been unsurpassable. In the niches of the tower we find portraits of Ludwig V, the great builder of the Castle and of youthful and elegant Friedrich V. There is also a memorial tablet dating from 1619. It says that Ludwig built this palace in 1533 and that Friedrich added to it the dining-hall and the statues, which are masterpieces by Sebastian Goetz.

At the western end of the Gun Park a memorial tablet reminds us of Goethe's seven visits to Heidelberg. The poem is by Marianne Willemer, a dancer who met Goethe in Heidelberg.

The Eastern Fortification: The "Powder Tower" (Krautturm)

We now walk back past the Bridge House towards the Powder Tower at the south-east corner of the Castle. The mighty tower got its name from the lower storey where the gunpowder was stored. This colossal building the walls of which are up to 6.50 metres thick, diameter 24 metres, restricted the blowing up by the French in 1689. Four years later they tried again but the tower only split in two parts. The blown-up part tumbled down into the moat and has permitted a free view into

After the blowing up in 1693 only the outer part of the Powder Tower tumbled down into the moat.

the three-storeyed tower with its vaults and central supports. The wooden ceilings had been replaced by stone vaultings when Friedrich IV built an octagonal storey on top of the tower in 1600.

Eastern flank of the Castle with Great Terrace. Between the octagonal Bell Tower and the Chemist's Tower are the rear façades of the Hall of Mirrors Building (with bay-window) and the Ottheinrich Building.

The loop-holes for fire-arms are still to be found and show us the purpose for which the romantic ruin had been built. Today, however, it is one of the most picturesque parts of the Castle. At the end of the moat is a roofed rampart.

The "Chemist's Tower" (Apothekerturm)

Like its neighbours, the Gun Tower and the Bell Tower, it dates back to the 15th century. In those times it was a two-storeyed building. From here the long eastern defensive line could be secured and it was also a good place for the rake of the Friesenberg. In 1600 Friedrich IV turned the loop-holes into windows and added three storeys to it. The lower storey, today the laboratory of the Pharmaceutical Museum, was the chemist's workshop.
Along the eastern flank roofed emplacements were built because the superstructed "Zwinger" had turned out to be useless for defence. The topped casemate in front of the Chemist's Tower was built after the Thirty Years' War. The façades between the Chemist's Tower and the Bell's Tower are only decorated by the Gothic bay-window at the gable of the Hall of Mirrors Building. The rear façade of the Ottheinrich Building, however, remained completely unadorned.

The Castle Gardens—"Hortus Palatinus"

Being a lover of the way of life of his times young Emperor Friedrich V, the "Winter King" wanted to adapt the northern and eastern surroundings of his Castle to his splendid princely household. So Salomon de Cause laid out a garden, the "Hortus Palatinus",

The "Hortus Palatinus" in 1620 before its completion and destruction in the Thirty Years' War (according to Th. Verhas).

which as the "Eighth Wonder of the World" attracted great attention in its times.

To the great disadvantage of the Castle's defence, Friedrich V blew up rocks and filled up the Friesen valley. Innumerable stairs connected the five terraces. Ponds, fountains, statues and grottoes were set up between flower beds and exotic trees. The orangery and the bitter orange garden were roofed over and heated in winter. In the "Great Grotto", in the corner of the terrace rare

"Father Rhine" on his stony bed. Fountains in front of the Great Grotto.

stones, corals, shells and fountains could be seen.

Around the portal various wild animals were arranged with the lion in the middle.

The smallest terrace on the top contained bath-houses and cabinets, an altan with reliefs and more than life-size statues of the builder and his wife. After 6 years the garden had been completed when the Thirty Years' War broke out. Severe fights

The Old Town between Castle and Neckar in springtime.

33

took place in it and at last it was damaged in part. During the following decades fruit and vegetables were grown in the former "Royal Garden". The statues were taken to Schwetzingen and Mannheim by Karl-Theodor, some of them even were found in the gardens of Heidelberg's citizens.

The former "Hortus Palatinus" was not reconstructed before 1803 when Heidelberg Castle and Town became a part of the country of Baden. Under the government of Karl Friedrich von Baden the gardens were laid out as you find them today.

Parts of it were turned into a botanic garden by the University.

1. Schloss, 2. Friedrichsbau, 3. Dicker Thurm, 4. Zeughaus, 5. Ballspielhaus, 6. Grosse-Fass-Gebäude, 7. Churfürstlicher Garten, 8. Pommeranzenbäume, 9. Herrengarten, 10. Altes Schloss, 11. Heiliggeistkirche, 12. Mönchhof, 13. Oberes Stadtthor, 14. St. Jacob, 15. Franziskaner Kirche, 16. Churfürstliche Kanzlei, 17. Churfürstliche Münze, 18. Zehnthaus, 19. Mantelthurm, 20. Churfürst-

It contains various foreign trees, shrubs and wide green lawns. This garden was one of the favourite places of 60 years old Goethe during his stay in Heidelberg. At the mountain side of the Great Terrace we find a picturesque corner with Goethe's stone bench and a memorial tablet to the great German poet.

At the end of the rock we again have a lovely view onto Old Heidelberg, the Neckar, the Karl's Gate, the sluice and especially the Neckar valley with the Castle ruins in front of it.

We now walk back along the upper part of the gardens and find ourselves at the end of our tour, just in front of the Castle gate.

licher Marstall, 21. Mittelthor, 22. Collegium Casimirianum, 23. Hexenthurm, 24. Augustinerkloster (Sapienz), 25. Grosses Contubernium, 26. Juristisches und medizinisches Auditorium, 27. Thurm mit Brückenaffe, 28. St. Peterskirche, 29. Schiessthor, 30. St. Annenkirchhof, 31. Trutzkaiser, 32. Exercierplatz, 33. Speyerer Thor, 34. Dominikanerkirche.

View over the Castle altan onto the Old Town and the Church of the Holy Ghost.

Round Old Heidelberg

Baroque Houses Set Upon Gothic Foundations

As a settlement of hunters, fishermen, craftsmen and tradesmen Heidelberg was not documented before 1196. In 1225 the Bishop of Worms gave the place to the Earls Palatine of the Rhine who made them their residence soon after. Slim Gothic mansions were built along the narrow lanes and squares keeping the town walls as short as possible. Later on gorgeous buildings in the Renaissance style were added to the panorama of the town.

After its destruction in 1689/93 the Castle has remained unchanged. The former Gothic town however which had been damaged almost entirely was reconstructed by its citizens. Only a few buildings have survived the Orleans War. According to a plan of Elector Johann Wilhelm, Heidelberg was to become a "modern" residence town in the Baroque style with a spacious Castle in the plain outside the town, broad streets and homogeneous houses. The citizens however wanted to rebuild their houses as fast and as cheaply as ever possible. Thus the old lower storeys were often built over, the narrow streets remained. Unadorned, simple houses with slim gables and narrow corridors leading to the outside stairs at the rear front were built in those times. A few decades later, however, the houses were set up in the Baroque style.

At the Karl's Square ("Karlsplatz")

Let us start our round walk at the car park which lies below the Castle in the Main-Street ("Hauptstrasse"). At the north side of the Karl's Square, below the stone monument of the Elector, is a broad building, the grand-ducal palace, built in 1717. It was the Heidelberg residence of the Dukes of Baden, in which the Academy of Sciences is housed today.

At the south-east corner of the Karl's Square we find two of Heidelberg's most famous historic students' inns, the "Seppl" and the "Roter Ochsen".

Historic student's inn at the Karl's Square.

A memorial tablet on the house opposite the grand-ducal palace, the Boisserée House, says that Goethe lived here in 1814 and 1815. It was here that the Boisserée brothers collected old German paintings. This complete collection of Romanticism has been transferred to Munich.

"Seppl", a historic students' inn at the Karlsplatz.

The Market Place ("Marktplatz")

Walking along the "Mönchsgasse" we reach the "Heiliggeist-strasse" and turn to our left. The "Nebelhaus" (1710) on the right side of the street is one of Heidelberg's oldest Baroque buildings. The street ends at the Market Place in the centre of which stands the Church of the Holy Ghost. On the opposite side is the Town Hall ("Rathaus"). This square was the place of public judgement and punishment in former centuries. In the 15th century trials for witchcraft were held in Heidelberg. Documents tell us about those times:

in 1525: "seven persons beheaded on the Market Place, three fingers cut off";

in 1572: under the government of Elector Friedrich III Super-intendent Sylvanus of Ladenburg was beheaded because of his religious conviction;

in 1812: Hölzerlipps, a captain of brigands, was condemned to death and beheaded in the western part of the town.

In 1600 the tragedy of two noble families of Heidelberg came to its end on the Market Place. During a banquet at the Elector's court two youthful friends, Hans von Handschuhsheim and Friedrich von Hirschhorn, fighted a duel on the Market Place. Both were the last ones of their families. Hans died of his wounds. His mother cursed the noble family of Hirschhorn which died out because Friedrich had no children. The tombstones of the Handschuhsheim family are to be seen in the St. Vitus Church in Handschuhsheim and are excellent masterpieces of this time.

Where the Hercules Fountain is situated today was the "Triller" up to 1740, a cage in which people were at show because of slight offences.

The Town Hall, built in 1701 with the Hercules Fountain in front of it.

On market days the square is full of stalls with flowers, fish, vegetables, etc.

The Market Place with the Hercules Fountain and the Gothic Church of the Holy Ghost.

The Town Hall ("Rathaus")

The Baroque centre of the building dates from the first years of Heidelberg's reconstruction about 1700. On the wall of the Great Hall is a painting which shows Elector Ottheinrich handing over the Reformation statutes to the rector of the University.

Daily at 7 p.m. the chimes of the Town Hall Tower can be heard. The best place for visitors who want to hear it is the Corn Market (Kornmarkt).

The Church of the Holy Ghost

In 1400 King Ruprecht I laid the foundation stone for this towering church which probably had two predecessors at the same place.

It is the largest Gothic church in the Palatine region and was the burial place of the electoral family as well as the festival hall of the University. It was not finished before 1544 when the tower was added to it. Slim buttresses emphasize the vertical lines as a symbol of worship.

The stalls round the church were already documented in 1483 when the University sold them to the town. The roof and the tower of the church are Baroque. On top of the water pipes are the heads of beasts of chase. Above the centre portal at the main street side of the church are the arms of Elector Johann Wilhelm and of his wife, of the noble family of Medici. On the house No. 190, opposite the church, on the former court pharmacy, is another gorgeous electoral coat of arms.

The Places of Burial of the Electors

We enter the church through a side portal at the west end of the nave. Epitaphs from four centuries are to be found on the walls. The unpretentious tomb of King Ruprecht I and his wife Elizabeth is the only one among 55 electoral tombs which has not been destroyed by French soldiers in 1693.

First they locked up several citizens in the church. The poor people were not freed before the roof had caught fire. Then General Melac's gang destroyed the tombs and epitaphs. According to a chronicle the dead bodies of the Electors were torn out of their tin coffins and thrown out into the street. The soldiers took the coffins with them as a loot.

Epitaph of King Ruprecht I and his wife (1410).

The "Bibliotheca Palatina" (The Palatine Library)

The choir of the church differs very much from the dark nave. Broad daylight breaks through the windows. In the galleries the extensive library was housed. The "Bibliotheca Palatina" had its origin in 1419 by the donation of a nobleman. In 1438 Ludwig III added to it his private collection of 152 volumes. At the same time the construction of the galleries in the Church of the Holy Ghost was planned. The Library's world-wide fame however refers to the donation of Ottheinrich and Huldrich Fugger who after his death added to it his own library of about 1000 pounds of weight.

The precious volumes lay on desks at everybody's disposal but were protected against theft by clasps. After storming Heidelberg in 1623 Duke Maximilian of Bavaria sent this precious collection to Rome, together with the University Library and the electoral private library. The passive resistance of the citizens however was unsuccessful: they hid all planks in the town. So crates were made out of desks and wooden ceilings, even wine vats were used for the transport of the irreplacable volumes. At last the boothy was carried to Italy on fifty carts. Most of it is in the possession of the Vatican today, some volumes were restored or bought back and are at show in the University Library, e.g. the famous Manesse-Manuscript.

Church of the Holy Ghost: nave with library choir.

The quarrel about the Church of the Holy Ghost

The history of the church has often been connected with the fate of Heidelberg town and Castle. The church was Catholic or Protestant, after the Elector's own religious confession. In 1705 it was even divided in two by a wall between the choir and the nave. When Elector Karl-Friedrich moved his court from Düsseldorf to Heidelberg he claimed the whole church for the Catholics. The choir alone appeared too small to him, he wanted the Protestants to yield the church as it had been the electoral court church and the place of burial of the Electors. The two parties were backed by several German princes so that a religious war was to break out. The Elector gave in at last and the wall which had been pulled down meanwhile was reconstructed.

Angels in the nave of the Church of the Holy Ghost, late Gothic paintings in the arched ceiling round the "Hole of Ascension".

Karl-Friedrich transferred his residence to Mannheim in 1720 where he set up a spacious palace. After the wall had been pulled down temporarily in 1886 it was not finally removed before 1936 when the Protestant Church bought the claim from the Catholic Church.

The Galleries and the Church Tower

Let us now climb the stairs of the tower where we reach the northern gallery half way up. In these rooms religious collections are at show today, originally the Palatine Library was housed here. From the look-out platform we enjoy a lovely view of the town and its surroundings: The Castle with its mighty western fortification, the Königstuhl (568 metres above sea-level) and the

mountain railway opposite the Heiligenberg, the Neckar river in its narrow bed and the Old Town with its maze of roofs, narrow streets and backyards.

Keystone in the choir, the Imperial Eagle of Ruprecht I.

The Renaissance "Haus zum Ritter" was the only patrician house which outlasted the Orleans War of Succession.

The "Ritter"

Adjoining the tower of the church is the Haspelgasse. It is from here that we have a lovely view of the "Hotel zum Ritter" in the Main-Street. Built by the Huguenot, Charles Belier in 1592, it was the only house which sustained the destructions in 1689/93. On the unadorned ground-floor outer walls were window-shutters which could also be used as counters for the cloth-merchants. Above it is the magnificent Renaissance façade which is said to be one of the finest in Germany. The knight's statue on top gave the mansion its name. The bay-windows are beautifully decorated with figures. In the arms and symbols on the left is the Aries (in French: bélier). They belong to the figures on the two upper storeys on the right. On the gable we find two Christian inscriptions: "Soli Deo Gloria" and: "Si Jehovah non aedificat domum, frustra laborant aedificantes eam." Between them however the gentile invitation: "Persista, invicta Venus."

At the north side of the Church of the Holy Ghost, at the Fish Market, we find a very beautiful group of figures in a niche of the Tratteur House. It gave the mansion its name: "Madonnenhaus."

The Old Bridge (Karl-Theodor-Bridge) ("Alte Brücke")

Walking along the Steingasse we reach the Neckar and its oldest bridge. The centre of the towers of the picturesque bridge gate dates from the medieval town fortress of the 13th century.

Together with the bridge Karl-Theodor set up a connecting building (1786–1788). The western tower contains three low, dark cellars, the eastern tower one cellar and the winding stairs. In the centre

The statue of the Holy Virgin at the Fish Market.

however are two light and sunny prison rooms with view onto the River, Castle and Town. Here the tardy debtors were imprisoned whereas criminals were locked up in the dungeons.

On a memorial tablet the Town of Heidelberg thanks the brave Austrians who defended the bridge against the French in 1799. Up to 1784 there was a roofed wooden bridge which was set upon pillars. The outer parts on both banks were drawbridges. Storms of war and innumerable floods however damaged no less than four bridges in the current of time. A massive quad-rangular tower built upon the second pillar was to protect the northern bridge-head.

Gate of the Old Bridge with Baroque spires seen from the river side: In front Karl-Theodor's statue with the river gods, on the left is the Neckar School.

View from the northern bank of the Neckar upon the Old Bridge and the Castle with the "Königstuhl" in the background.

The statue on the town side shows Karl-Theodor. Four allegorical figures symbolize the regions which were in possession of the House of Wittelsbach: the Rhine, Danube, Neckar and Moselle. The latin inscription says that the memorial was set up in 1788 by the Council and Town of Heidelberg in honour of Karl-Theodor, the "Father of all Palatines". On the north side is Pallas Athene— goddess of Wisdom and patron goddess of castles and towns, below her are Piety, Justice, Agriculture and Commerce, then come Astronomy, Architecture, Painting, Sculpture and Music.

The statue of Nepomuk, the patron saint of bridges, has been transferred to the northern bank of the Neckar.

In the double house west of the bridge gate was the "Neckar School" (1706) which has already been documented in the 16th century. The coats of arms on the western wing belong to the butchers' guild house and the slaughter-house. Through the "Tränktor" the cattle was driven to the watering-place in the Middle Ages.

The Lower Street ("Untere Strasse")

The Baroque mansion "Cajeth" in 12, Haspelgasse stands on the place the ancient merchants' and dancing-hall was once situated. At the historic Student's inn "Knösel" we turn into the "Untere Strasse". On our right, in the "Pfaffengasse", we find the native place of Friedrich Ebert who was German President from 1919 to 1925. The palais No. 11 Untere Strasse was built by the electoral masterbuilder Rischer in 1711 for his own family. At the beginning of the 19th century the building was used as a University fencing-room. At the Hay Market ("Heumarkt") with its romantic bay-window above the Cafe Scheu we follow the Grosse Mantelgasse downhill.

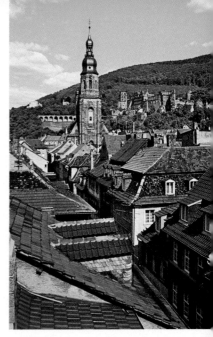

A lane in the Old Town near the Church of the Holy Ghost.

On the Banks of the Neckar

On our left is a bulky, unadorned building, called the "Heuscheuer". It was built in the 18th century of the ruins of a tower which had been damaged in 1693. Here the food reserves and the deliveries of products of nature were stored. Today this ancient building contains modern lecture-rooms.

Behind it is a fortress-like block of houses, the "Marstall". The remaining buildings once stood outside the ancient town walls

The Arsenal, adjoining to the left the Haystack.

and were used as an arsenal. The former "Royal Stables" are only to be seen in a picture by Merian (1620): a gorgeous seven-storied Renaissance building stood on the southern end of the courtyard where today the modern University building is. Like so many other buildings it was destroyed in the Orleans War of Succession in 1689/93. The arsenal (1510) the northern walls of which once have been "flowed round by the waves of the Neckar" still remains. The dining-hall of the University is housed in it today.

The Main-Street ("Hauptstrasse")

On the site of a former Dominican monastery (founded in 1476) on the left are the School of Anatomy and the Friedrich Building of the University, built in the 19th century.

The building opposite the Main-Street façade of the Friedrich Building was built in 1707 of blown-up rocks of the Thick Tower. The more than life-size figure of the builder gave the mansion its name "The Giant" (Zum Riesen). A tablet tells us of Kirchhoff, who, together with Bunsen, discovered the spectrum analysis. In the front of the Friedrich Building stands Bunsen's memorial. Let us now follow the Main-Street towards the Castle. On the right, in No. 16, Märzgasse is the house where Max Wolf, the founder of Heidelberg's Observatory lived (1863–1932). The world-famed astronomer discovered a photographical method of star-observation. In the backyard of 16, Märzgasse his private observatory is still to be seen. The Baroque palais next to it, No. 18, was in the possession of Graf von Wieser and was lived in by the famous lawyer von Vangerow from 1840 to 1870. Following the Landfried- and Karl-Ludwig-Strasse we reach the Main-Street in front of the Providence Church ("Provindenzkirche"). Set upon an electoral court garden in 1660 it was rebuilt after the destruction in 1693. Its name is derived from Karl-Ludwig's motto: "Dominus providebit."

The mansion "Zum Riesen" with a statue of the Builder.

The Palatine Museum "Kurpfälzisches Museum"

About 1710 the "Palais Moras" was built, a distinguished mansion, now in No. 97, Main-Street. Its builder was a high official at court and a professor of law. Courtyard and garden have perfectly preserved their picturesque beauty. In the interior with its ancient Baroque stucco ceilings the collection of the Palatine Museum is housed the founder of which was Karl Graf von Graimberg. Here the visitor can find paintings and copperplate engravings showing the Castle and its Electors, a plaster-cast of the lower jaw bone of the "Homo heidelbergensis", the oldest European human find. There are also Roman stone tablets and two complete tombs of

Riemenschneider-altar in the Palatine Museum: the "Windsheim Altar of the Twelve Apostles".

the time about 600 p. Chr. n. The most precious work of art however is the 16th century "Windsheim Altar" by Tilman Riemenschneider. At the Schiffgasse our eyes are caught by the richly decorated bay-window and the portal of the two cinemas. After its destruction in 1693 parts of the medieval "Wormser Hof", the palais of the Bishops of Worms, have been included in the present building.

Seven fine statues in the centre of the shrine and impressing half-reliefs on the wings show Jesus Christ amidst his disciples.

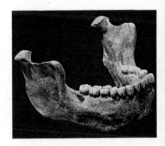

Lower-jaw bone of the "Homo heidelbergensis" (500 000 a. Chr. n.) (original).

49

The University Quarter ("Universitätsviertel")

The Schiffgasse near the Main-Street.

At the University Square: On the left is the Old University, on the right is the "New University", built in 1931.

In the Grabengasse we leave the Main-Street and find ourselves in the University Square. The land from here to the Bismarck Square was called the "Fore Town" in former centuries. Behind the Lion's Fountain ("Löwenbrunnen") is the Old University. Pope Urban IV had permitted the establishment of "General Studies" in a document on July 24th in 1386. Elector Ruprecht I gave the University its charter of the constitution which was being read annually to the citizens on 1st November in the Church of the Holy Ghost. It granted safe-conduct and exemption from taxation to all professors, students, booksellers and clerks. It was because of the outstanding international reputation of Magister Marsilius, the first rector of Germany's oldest University, that

*The Great Hall ("Aula") of the Old University, redecorated in 1886.
The painting shows Athene's entrance to Heidelberg.*

in the first year over 500 students came to Heidelberg. Due to the
wars in the 17th century the University lost much of its fame. It was
Markgraf Karl-Friedrich von Baden who, in 1805, brought the
University to new life again.
He re-established it, and in honour of this Prince and of Ruprecht I
who founded it the University was called "Ruperto Carola".

The Students' Prison ("Studentenkarzer")

On the rear façade of the Old University you should visit the
rooms of the Students' Prison.
It was used from 1712 to 1914 when the jurisdiction over the
students was the right of the University administration.
Because of drunkennesses, gross misdetablo or disturbances the
students were imprisoned up to two weeks, quarrels with the

police were punished with four weeks. These offences were taken easy by the students and each of them wanted to be imprisoned at least once in his student life. After two or three days with nothing but water and bread the inhabitants were allowed to attend the lectures and to receive food from outside. The names of the rooms like "Grand Hotel", "Sanssouci" and "Throne Hall"—for the toilet—give evidence of the inhabitants' sense of humour.

The "New University" was built in 1931 but today many of the University buildings are no longer in the old part of the town. Modern buildings have been set up in the "Neuenheimer Feld" on the right hand bank of the Neckar.

A room in the Students' prison with "paintings" and inscriptions by the inhabitants.

At the corner of the Grabengasse and the "Plöck" stands the University Library which was built in 1905. Its famous manuscript collections are part of the "Bibliotheca Palatina". About 890 manuscripts, most of them in Old German, have been restored by the Vatican. The most valuable manuscript is the "Manesse-Codex", which was in possession of Friedrich IV and bought from the Paris Library in 1888.

The predecessor of the Church of St. Peter opposite has first been documented in 1316. It used to be Heidelberg's parish church although it was situated outside the town walls. Up to the 15th century the Church of the Holy Ghost was inferior to St. Peter's Church. In 1400 King Ruprecht I gave the smaller church to the "rector, doctors and masters of art" of the University. The present building dates back to the 15th century. The one-naved interior was once without pillars which have been added to it in the 19th century.

In the small churchyard and on the outer and inner church walls are grave-stones of professors and famous citizens, among them is also the tombstone of Olympia Fulvia Morata (died in 1555), the first lady professor in Europe.

The Jesuit Quarter ("Jesuitenviertel")

In the Grabengasse, at the rear façade of the New University stands a building in the shape of a horse-shoe, the "Collegium Academicum". The former seminary of the Jesuits which was built in 1750 has since served many purposes: as lunatic asylum, as a students' dwelling-house, etc. The building opposite was a Jesuit High School.

Over a short flight of steps we reach the University courtyard. In its south-west corner stands the Witches Tower (Hexenturm), the last remains of the old fortification. It was built in 1380 and was once a women's prison. A second flight of steps and a passage to the right lead us to the Church of the Jesuits. It was planned by the Baroque master-builder Breunig in 1712.

The northern façade is designed in the "Jesuit Style"

The Witches Tower in the courtyard of the New University, once part of the old town fortification.

Interior of the Church of the Jesuits, the nave and the High Altar.

with statues of Ignatius of Loyola. In its vaults the church contains the body of Friedrich I the Victorious. Adjoining the church in the east is the mighty Jesuit monastery. In a niche on the west side of the church, No. 2 Schulstrasse, a beautiful statue of the Holy Virgin strikes our eyes, a work of art by Peter van den Brandens.

The Corn Market ("Kornmarkt")

Following the Heugasse we again reach the main street and turn right. The "Medersche Haus" at the corner of the Kettengasse is regarded as a typical 18th century mansion. The narrow gable front is decorated with beautiful reliefs and a charming figure of the Holy Virgin.

Off Market Square in the Mittelbadgasse and Oberbadgasse were once Heidelberg's medieval "bath-houses".

The "Prinz Carl" opposite the Town Hall was a first-class hotel in the 19th century. In 1849 it was the headquarters of the Revolutionary Army, and only a year later Prince Wilhelm of Prussia, the later Emperor Wilhelm I, took his own camp-bed with him. Famous guests like Bismarck (in 1856), Emperor Friedrich III, son of Wilhelm I, his wife Victoria (in 1860), Mark Twain (in 1874) and Moltke (in 1876) give evidence of the world-wide fame of the hotel which was shut down in 1915.

The "Corn Market Madonna" by Peter van Brandens with the Castle ruins in background is one of Heidelberg's most picturesque motives for photographers. In the house No. 5 Corn Market lived Graf von Graimberg, the founder of the Palatine Museum. Only a few steps further we find ourselves back in the Market Square, the starting-point of our round.

An evening at the Corn Market: the Holy Virgin by Peter van den Brandens in front of the Castle ruins.

An Excursion

If you are not too exhausted let us follow the Main-Street to the Karl's Square ("Karlstor"). Passing by the "Seppl" and the "Roter Ochsen" we reach the "Plankengasse" the prolongation of which is called the "Eselspfad". It was formerly a junction between the "Herrenmühle" – which has been burnt down meanwhile – and the Castle. Today it is a blind alley. The "Buhlsche Haus" with its large-scale flight of steps and the "Palais Weimar" opposite date from the early 18th century. The "Friesenberg" is a way up to the Castle along the Friesen valley or through the Scheffel Terrace inside the Castle gardens. The Karl's Gate is the final point of the Main-Street, it was built in the style of the "Early Classicism". Karl-Theodor, the builder of the Great Vat, the Old Bridge and the Schwetzingen Castle gardens built it in 1775 as a part of the eastern town fortification. In each cellar and upper storey were three prison rooms, in the ground-floor were the rooms of the guardians. Due to the "Wehrsteig" the Karl's Square is a good starting-point for walks along the opposite bank of the Neckar, especially the Hirschgasse and of Heidelberg's most famous lane, the Philosophen Lane ("Philosophenweg").

View from the "Philosophengärtchen" onto the Neckar, Old Town and Castle.

On the right of the Neckar

The Philosophen Lane ("Philosophenweg")

The easiest way to get there is either over the Old Bridge or following the Bridge Street ("Brückenstrasse"). Coming from the Bismarck Square we walk over the Theodor-Heuss-Bridge and turn right to the Bergstrasse. This is where the Philosophen Lane starts. A magnificent view of the town recompenses the effort of walking up here. Beautiful gardens invite you to sit down and rest for a while. There are also marked foot-paths for long or short walks in the surrounding country.

Handschuhsheim

Over the Theodor-Heuss-Bridge we reach the quarters Neuenheim and Handschuhsheim. At the end of the Steubenstrasse stands the Church of St. Vitus ("Sankt-Vitus-Kirche"), the oldest church of the town, built in the 11th century. Its predecessor has already been documented in the 8th century.

The mural paintings of the 15th century tell us about Christ's passion. Of interest are the tombstones especially four epitaphs: In a chapel which was once the choir are figures of the noble family of Handschuhsheim. The inscription says that Hans von Handschuhsheim was killed in a duel on the Market Square at the age of 15, a short time after the death of his sister Barbara. The memorial opposite shows the parents, Heinrich von Handschuhsheim and

Amale Beusser von Ingelheim with Barbara and Hans. This epitaph is without an inscription.

The other double epitaph — Hans von Ingelheim and Margareth von Handschuhsheim (1519) — is a masterpiece of a late Gothic sculptor. The Steubenstrasse ends near the "Tiefburg", the Castle of the Nobles of Handschuhsheim. It was built in the 13th century and gravely damaged during the War of Succession in 1689/93.

Double epitaph of Hans von Handschuhsheim and his sister (1600).

The "Tiefburg", the Castle of the Nobles of Handschuhsheim.

The Holy Mountain ("Heiligenberg")

The way up to the Holy Mountain is easily to be found on the right of the "Tiefburg". There is a large information tablet at the car park on the Holy Mountain. A few metres back the road we find the foundations of the monastery of St. Stephanus with its chapel. It was built in 1090 by monks of St. Michael's Church and fell into disrepair in the 16th century.

Out of its stones the look-out tower was built from which we enjoy a marvellous view of Heidelberg.

The "Heidenloch" on the other side of the street is 55 metres deep and at its botton laid with Roman bricks. It is probably of Celtic origin as only a settlement could have needed such a lot of water.

On our way to the peak of the Holy Mountain we follow the main path. Memorial stones remind us of the Celts who lived in this region about 500—100 a. Chr. n.

For their defence they built a fortress on the peak of the mountain which

Look-out tower on the Holy Mountain.

in peace times was occupied by soldiers only, in was times however provided room enough for the whole race. The walls were of sandstone blocks with wooden balustrades, behind them stones and soil were raised and strengthened by a wooden construction.

Two ring walls surrounded the two peaks of the mountain, the outer being 3 kilometres long with two passages in each of them.

The gates were strengthened by trunks, a double wall in the interior provided more safety to the inhabitants.

The foundations of St. Michael's Church still remain almost completely and give an impressing idea of the construction of the monastery which was founded by monks of Lorsch in 870.

In the 11th century it was altered to a Romanic Basilica

Ruins of the monastery of St. Michael (9th century) on the Holy Mountain. The basilica was left by the monks in 1503.
(Freig. d. Reg. Karlsruhe 0/8279)

and dedicated to All Saints. This is where the name of the mountain came from. After some monks had been killed by stones of the collapsing tower the others left the buildings in 1503.

The imposing new "Feierstätte" which was built in 1935 by the "Arbeitsdienst" was to be used as a "Germanic Festival Place" but it looks like an amphitheatre and is scarcely used today.

The Neuenheimer Feld

On our way back to Heidelberg we pass the "Tiefburg" once more and follow the road No. B3 towards the City. At the bifurcation we turn left to the broad "Berliner Strasse" which leads us to the Neuenheimer Feld with its modern clinic buildings of Heidelberg University. After the "Ernst-Walz-Bridge" you either turn left to the town center or you go straight ahead to the Federal Centre of Sports ("Bundesleistungszentrum") and the municipal open-air swimming-pool, the youth hostel and the Botanic Garden.

The mountain railway at the Königstuhl opposite the Holy Mountain with its famous Philosophen Lane.

Heidelberg with the Königstuhl (568 m). The vast view of the Neckar valley and over the mountains of the Odenwald.

(Freig. d. Reg. Karlsruhe 0/7699)

The Königstuhl

The electric mountain railway with its station at the Corn Market (opposite the "Parkhaus") takes you to the Castle in two minutes and to the "Molkenkur" in five minutes. Up to 1537 stood here the "Upper Castle" with the gunpowder arsenal of the Castle.
A flash of lightning blew off the gunpowder and destroyed the "Upper Castle".
In the 19th century a house for the medical treatment with whey ("Molke") was set upon the plateau. The owner kept 50 goats. There is a famous look-out restaurant on the same place today, the "Molkenkur-Restaurant".
From here it is easy for you to get to the top of the mountain, the "Königstuhl", 568 metres above sea-level, either on foot, by car or by the electric mountain railway. From the tower there is a magnificent view out over the Rhine Plain. The "Childrens' Paradise" ("Kinderparadies"), the Observatory ("Sternwarte") and romantic foot-paths are the main objects of interest on top of the Königstuhl.

Stone signposts help the wanderer to keep the right direction. A pleasant way up to the Königstuhl starts in the Old Town via the Castle or the "Klingteich" near the Church of St. Peter.

Two foot-paths are crossing the motorway-tunnel: The Wolf-höhlenweg starts at the Municipal Garden ("Stadtgarten"), the beginning of the Riesensteinweg is near the Märzgasse. Two sandstone rocks are lying on the path. The story goes that once upon a time two giants tried to throw rocks over the Neckar. One of them, the father, threw his rock as far as the Gaisberg. His son however hit the father's rock and rammed it into the ground.

The mountain between the Gaisberg (375 metres above sea-level) and the Königstuhl is called "Sprunghöhe" and leads you along the Exotic Garden with its ancient mammoth trees towards the log-house which is the starting-point of many rambles in the surrounding country. The rhododendron garden nearby is an attractive place in spring-time.

Near the Speyerer's Hof Hospital an impressing War Cemetery was laid out for the soldiers of World War I and II. The hills of the "Kohlhof" are—for a few days in winter—Heidelberg's skiing-grounds.

Along the Neckar valley

10 kilometres upstream is the charming city of Neckargemünd, the ancient Free Town at the mouth of the river Elsenz. It was from here that General Tilly besieged in vain the fortress of Dilsberg in 1622. Dilsberg Castle once belonged to the Earls of Elsenzgau, in the 13th century it was handed over the Palatinate. A subterranean foot-path leads the visitors to the bottom of a more than 100 metres deep draw-well in the castle courtyard. From this castle which is set upon the top of a steep hill the glance sweeps over the hills of the Odenwald and the Neckar valley with Neckarsteinach, the "City of the Four Castles". The most famous of them is a castle named "Schadeck" which is also known as "Schwalbennest". It was from here that in the Middle Age the robber-knight Bligger von Steinach held up the merchants on their way to Heidelberg by means of chains which he stretched across the river. Thus he was nicknamed "Landschad". Hans Bligger II Landschad von Steinach however was also a poet who lived in the 13th century. The epitaphs of other members of the "Landschad" family are to be found in the Protestant Church of Neckarsteinach. The Burgenstrasse on the right bank of the Neckar leads us to Hirschhorn. Hirschhorn Castle was once the dwelling of the rich Nobles of Hirschhorn. You can find their epitaphs in the Carmelitan

The Neckar river passing by the Odenwald mountains east of Heidelberg.

Church and in the Ersheim Chapel on the opposite bank of the river. The last one of this family was Friedrich von Hirschhorn who as a youngster killed his friend Hans von Handschuhsheim in a duel

The romantic City of Neckargemünd at the mouth of the river Elsenz.

The ancient fortress of Dilsberg set upon the mountain above the Neckar even resisted Tilly's attacks.

The four castles of the "Landschad von Steinach" family whose fine tombstones are to be seen in the Protestant Church of Neckarsteinach.
The ancient castle above the city of Hirschhorn was lived in by the Nobles of Hirschhorn up to the 17th century.

The idyllic City of Eberbach surrounded by the Odenwald mountains on the banks of the Neckar.

and was cursed by the dead boy's mother. All his children died young.

Zwingenberg Castle, a little further upstream near Eberbach, also belonged to the Hirschhorn family.

One of his many sons had almost reached the age of an adult when he was killed in Heidelberg during a riot. The middle part of the Castle with its mighty tower dates back to the 12th century, the stately palace was renewed in 1583.

Zwingenberg Castle, some miles upstream Eberbach, also belonged to the noble family of Hirschhorn.

Zwingenberg Castle on the banks of the Neckar.

Schwetzingen

The mosque in the garden of the castle of Schwetzinger reflected in the dreamy pond.

South-west of Heidelberg is the little town of Schwetzingen which is particularly famous for its asparagus. Here the world-famed Electoral Castle gardens were laid out in the 18th century. After the destruction of the former garden in the Thirty Years' War and in the Orlean's War of Succession the present Castle was begun in 1699. The spacious park was laid out by Karl-Theodor in the style of Versailles with its intricate geometrical design. Not far from Schwetzingen is Mannheim with its mighty Rococo castle and the city of Speyer with its ancient Romanic Emperor's Cathedral (11th century).

The lighted castle should remind us of the great fires during the wars of succession and of the lightning of 1764.